GW00600615

CAUTION !
USED CARS

A STEP BY STEP GUIDE TO
BUYING A BETTER USED CAR
AND SELLING THE ONE YOU OWN

Philip D. Turner

Published in 1991 by
The Self Publishing Association Ltd
18 High Street
Upton-upon-Severn, Worcs.
A MEMBER OF

in conjunction with
PHILIP D. TURNER

British Library Cataloguing in Publication Data

A catalogue record for this book is
available from the British Library

ISBN   1 85421 137 4 (Paperback)
        1 85421 121 8 (Hardback)

Designed and Produced by The Self Publishing Association Ltd
Printed and Bound in Great Britain by Billing & Sons Ltd, Worcester

CONTENTS

AUTHOR'S NOTE

It is important to stress that a book of this nature has not been without its preparation difficulties: the main ones being that many aspects relating to a car's overall condition (be they structural, mechanical, electrical or otherwise) cannot always be dealt with coherently or in a convenient, straightforward fashion. For this reason there may be cross-referencing to – and possibly some repetition of – topics in other sections where considered appropriate.

Also this book does not set out to cover every examinable detail of a car – there are simply too many of them with too many variations of vehicle to make this practicable. Therefore, you would be wise to heed any other valuable advice from as many other relavant sources to compensate for this.

In addition to this, and whilst packed with advice from many professional sources, it remains the final decision of the author as to what has been included. To this end it is not inconceivable that some readers may disagree with some of the content.

The author accepts no responsibility for any damages or losses incurred to or by any person or vehicle arising from their acting on any technical or other information disclosed throughout this guide.

ACKNOWLEDGEMENTS

I should like to express my gratitude to the following people for their role in the preparation of this book:

My girlfriend, Olga Grauss – for providing unlimited encouragement and critical feedback.

My Mum, Doris Turner – also for her support.

E & G Car Sales Ltd., (Lee Green, SE12) – for providing the initial inspiration for the text.

Bob McCready – for much needed clerical help.

And to everyone who has imparted helpful advice of either a practical or technical nature and particularly in the early stages, I extend a thank you to John Cufley (Bexley Auto Repairs) and to Frank Molda.

Some of the material in Chapters 6 and 8 has been derived from a book by John Pritchard entitled *The Motorist and the Law – A guide to Motorist's Rights*. (Penguin 1987). I am indebted to that book for its clear approach to an otherwise tricky subject, and I thoroughly recommend the purchase of it to read in conjunction with a guide such as *Caution! Used Cars*. Mr Pritchard's book also explores a diversity of legal situations which frequently relate to many motorists.

INTRODUCTION

Purpose Of This Book

This book is intended to help you make the right choice when buying a secondhand car, and is aimed mainly at those of you who are non-mechanics. I hope to prove that by following a step-by-step approach, you can confidently choose the most suitable car for your needs, and avoid the costly mistake of buying a bad one.

It is not intended as a mechanics' manual, nor will it burden you with over-complicated and unnecessary technical jargon. The need for such a guide arose in fact from the time I was looking to buy my second car and realised, to my despair, that genuine and inexpensive sources of good advice were quite thin on the ground. The advice I ended up with was of the kind that most used car-seeking people seem to get at one time or another: too technical to understand and remember, or full of half-truths and half-baked theories from enthusiastic would-be mechanics who often disappeared when their help was needed most.

For many of you who already know some of what to look for in a used car – and quite likely have a practised routine – let this book serve both as a useful reminder to what you already know and as a basis from which to broaden your knowledge for next time.

This book will show you:

* THE BEST TIME TO BUY SECONDHAND AND HOW TO RAISE THE MONEY (Chapter 1)

* HOW TO CHOOSE THE RIGHT CAR FOR YOU (Chapter 1)

* WHAT YOU CAN EXPECT FROM A USED CAR AND WHY IT IS IMPORTANT TO KNOW ITS HISTORY (Chapter 2)

* WHAT A PRICE GUIDE WILL TELL YOU (Chapters 2, 8 and 10)

* HOW TO CHECK THE STRUCTURAL AND MECHANICAL SOUNDNESS OF A CAR AND WHERE TO LOOK FOR ADDITIONAL SOURCES OF HELP (Chapters 3 and 5)

* HOW TO TEST DRIVE A USED CAR (Chapter 4)

* YOUR LEGAL RIGHTS WHEN BUYING SECONDHAND AND WHAT TO DO WHEN THE SELLER WILL NOT HELP (Chapter 6)

* HOW TO COPE WITH DEALERS AND SALES TALK (Chapter 7)

* HOW TO TRADE AT AUCTIONS (Chapter 8)

* EIGHT THINGS YOU MUST DO IMMEDIATELY UPON BUYING A USED CAR *IF YOU WANT TO SAVE MONEY* (Chapter 9)

* HOW TO SELL YOUR EXISTING CAR MORE QUICKLY AND PROFITABLY USING PROVEN TECHNIQUES, AND ALSO THE LEGAL OBLIGATIONS THAT BIND YOU (Chapter 10)

Happy hunting

Philip Turner, May 1991

Chapter 1

WHEN, HOW AND WHAT TO BUY

1.1   State Of The Secondhand Market

At the end of 1989 the Department of Transport reported a figure of over 24,000,000 vehicles on Britain's roads, of which some 19,720,000 were cars. The majority of cars are secondhand and the market is steadily increasing year by year.

Secondhand car sales are big business; thousands change hands every day of the week, through both private sales and car dealers. The Motor Trade, and in particular the used car trade, does not enjoy the best of reputations amongst the general public but it would be fair to say that this is the fault of a minority of bad dealers. The vast majority are honest and reliable. The problem for the customer is knowing who are the few that should be avoided, and eliminating unnecessary risk.

There are several reasons why buying a used car can be a gamble, and most relate to attempts by previous owners to save money. Successive owners – less likely than the original buyer to be able to afford full maintenance – may take the attitude that all but essential repairs can wait, or extend the service interval, or go to the wrong people for help. All this can have a telling effect on the car's long-term performance.

In fact, it is usually very difficult to know a car's true 'history'; in other words, the way in which it has been driven and looked after. While it is true that in the course of everyday driving a fair percentage of cars suffer bodywork damage through accident or carelessness, and that some will be totally written off in a serious collision, there is no other reason why a car bought brand new cannot last a good fifteen years or more in sound mechanical and driveable condition, irrespective of the number of previous owners. Study carefully the next time you see an early 1970's car in good condition which appears to be driving well – there are a few around, but should such longevity be that remarkable?

1.2   Best Times To Buy

The motor trade most definitely responds to seasonal fluctuations. The Motor Show in the autumn, for instance, tempts many people to buy earlier than they usually need and this creates a better than average selection of used cars for sale. The same is true of early August when newly registered cars are launched.

Most secondhand buying is done in the spring and summer when lighter evenings afford better viewing opportunities, and people are beginning to think more about day trips and summer holidays. For these reasons prices are generally higher than at other times of the year; salesman take advantage of the public willingness to buy.

Seasonal change also influences the sale of certain types of car. The sale of sporty models and convertibles, for instance, can boom at the first suggestion of warm weather.

Winter is therefore the better time to buy, if only because cars are cheaper now. Christmas preparations, poor weather and a general lack of incentive to drive for pleasure lead to fewer cars being sold and therefore prices will be more negotiable.

1.3 Raising The Money

There are several recognised means of raising money to buy a car and the merits of each, depending on personal circumstances, are reviewed below:

Savings:

This is old-fashioned but probably the best way to buy a large item since you (1) have the money ready, (2) get to own the car immediately and (3) do not have to pay any interest.

Loans/Overdraft:

Unless you know when you'll have the funds in to replenish a loan, you will be paying dearly to borrow. Always agree a sum with your bank or building society first, since the interest rates on agreed compared with unauthorised overdrafts are different (typically by around 1%). Other loans from banks and building societies can come in the form of a personal loan and are usually subject to earnings and status. Some offer tailored 'car loan' packages and possibly preferential rates to branch customers. Even if you are not a member of that bank or building society you can still be tempted with generous incentives which might include a free one-year breakdown subscription with a main motoring organisation; premium discounts from particular insurance companies, and/or discounts from tyre, battery and exhaust suppliers. Some packages will be more suitable than others so it is worth getting plenty of quotes.

Finance groups offer loans at various rates of repayment, some requiring collateral e.g. a house, in the case of a secured loan; however, some do offer unsecured loans but with higher repayment premiums. You can find details of these companies in both the local and national press.

If you are considering a loan remember that there are two different rates of interest and you should understand the difference between them. The flat rate (based on bank base rates) which is the most often quoted, is subject to fluctuation. The other, Annual Percentage Rate or APR, is the rate that you will actually repay. It is a compounded package fixed for the duration of the loan, e.g. 12, 24, 36 months.

Some secondhand dealerships offer 0% finance lending which might be a good idea if you can still get a sizeable discount and then repay over a fairly long period. There is also the possibility of borrowing from a group like the AA and you don't even have to be a member to apply for their 'motor loan' package.

Immediate Family:

Consider the possibility of borrowing from family or friends. You could offer to repay them in instalments as you would a bank or building society except at lower interest. In this way you both benefit: you with cheaper (and possibly more flexible) borrowing and they by getting some return on the money they lent you.

1.4   Choosing A Car To Suit Your Needs

What kind of car do you really need? This may be altogether different from the car you would really like and, for the majority of people at least, the choice will be something of a compromise. Today there are many different models of a similar type available and often little to choose between them.

The following are some of the main factors you may be considering:- purchase price – size of car (saloon or estate) – use (family, business or sports) – engine size – comfort – running costs (including insurance) – resale value – annual mileage and the possibility of longer journeys, especially continental travel – the length of time that you plan to keep the car.

Some of these factors will be more obvious, such as the size of car needed; others will require further examination.

> **Be wary of choosing a car on the basis of an image you want to project. Choosing an expensive car or one in poor condition can cost you a fortune.**

1.5 Engine Size And Comfort

Do you *need* that 3-litre gas guzzler to get you down to the shops and back? If you do you will be getting no more than about 15-16 mpg in town traffic even with the benefit of a tuned engine. On the other hand, if you do a lot of long distance motorway driving, and possibly overseas trips, is it really practical to buy a 1-litre Metro or Fiesta – and there are some with GB nationality plates! While appearing to give a saving on petrol, these cars would give you a less comfortable ride at speed over long distances than the more robust, deluxe Ford (Granada), Volvo or Mercedes designs which, along with their greater weight, have vastly improved suspension, longer wheelbase, better seating and more sophisticated extras. Also, larger engines tend on average to last longer than small ones because they run at lower revs.

An automatic gear-box may be worth serious consideration if your driving is mainly in urban areas. There is a small but significant fuel consumption penalty (approximately 15%) but it is also worth remembering that an automatic gear-box is often able to select the correct gear more quickly than can be done by the average driver and this often counteracts any tendency for higher fuel consumption. Automatic gear-boxes are more expensive to replace. On the other hand there is no clutch to wear out and be replaced and automatic gear-boxes are now very reliable.

1.6   Running Costs

> While considering how much you should pay for your next used car, remember that the initial outlay is not a very good indication of what the car is likely to cost to run. You should especially beware of picking up a large or deluxe car cheaply only to discover that it consumes vast quantities of petrol or that replacement parts are either hard to come by or very expensive.

Many people considering buying a second car tend to look for something quite small, leaving the larger, more powerful family car for heavier duties. The smaller one, which will be doing a lower mileage, is usually ideal for round town, stop-start traffic, and easy parking. If this is the kind of thing you have in mind, you might consider one of the smaller, mass produced hatchbacks which are relatively cheap to service and maintain, and also require lower insurance premiums.

Cars with good aerodynamic shapes are better on fuel

economy than taller, bulky or 'square' shaped cars. Remember that even a roof rack causes aerodynamic drag, adding around 4% to your fuel bill. Note also that the larger-engined version of a particular model may not necessarily use significantly more fuel than the smaller version, especially if you often carry passengers and baggage – the larger-engine is working less hard for any given speed. Check the car handbook or the Department of Energy's fuel consumption figures. Regular servicing, correct front wheel alignment and correct tyre pressures of the larger-engined model can offset a m.p.g advantage of an inadequately maintained smaller engine.

1.7   Insurance Group

In assessing initial costs, consider the likely insurance group rating that the car will be assigned to. You can find this out from a good price guide but remember that insurance ratings not only vary from company to company, but are subject to more complex factors such as age and experience of driver, personal driving record and even the area of the country where you live and intend to use the car, e.g. whether you are in a metropolitan area or deep in the countryside. Engine size will play a part in this and larger-bodied cars are looked upon as more likely to be involved in a collision. Also, newness, present value and the type of use to which the car will be put – social and domestic or business – will affect the insurance premium you'll pay.

Fuel-injected and turbo-charged engines can vastly increase your premiums. You would do well to obtain quotes from several companies before deciding the best deal. It may even pay you to go direct with the company, since in this way you could cut out much of the insurance broker fee and make yourself a considerable saving.

There are nine insurance groups to which a car may belong and these chiefly relate to some of the above factors including: size of car and engine, popularity, trim level and, among other things, ease of obtaining spares.

An example from each group is given below:

Group 1: Citroen 2-CV 6 'dolly' saloon
Group 2: Fiat Panda '4 x 4' 3-door hatchback
Group 3: Ford Cortina 1.6 L estate

Group 4: Austin Maestro 1.6 HL hatchback

Group 5: Ford Sierra Sapphire 2-litre GL saloon

Group 6: Renault 21 turbo 2-litre 5-speed saloon

Group 7: Ford Capri 2.8i fastback

Group 8: BMW 325i SE automatic saloon

Group 9: Porche 911 Carrera Sport Cabriolet.

1.8   Types Of Car Design And General Considerations

Essentially, there are four categories of car design: Saloon cars and hatchbacks; estate cars (or station wagons); sports cars and sports saloons, and convertibles. Your choice will depend on your needs but there is overlap in some of these categories; for example a sports saloon hatchback may well give you good performance, four or five seats and some of the benefits of an estate (opening rear hatch, fold-down rear seats). Some non-hatchback saloons also give you folding and split rear seats, so there is quite a variety of choice in model types and you may find that you don't have to make much of a compromise.

> **With estate cars in particular you need to examine the roof/roof-rack guttering: checking for dents, nicks, scratches and rust there could tell you that the car has had previous use as a 'workhorse'.**

Check also for leaks at the tailgate hinge. Once you have permission, a simple test worth doing is to throw a bucket of water or hose over the area and watch for leaks.

If you are thinking of buying a convertible, look closely for signs of the hood leaking (either currently or in the past) as this can cause serious floorpan/chassis corrosion. Check also that the hood lowers and raises easily and that all fixings and studs are satisfactory. Replacement hoods are readily available though, from specialist hood manufacturers with prices starting at about £650. Convertibles are more prone to vandalism and possible theft so where you live and park may have a bearing on your purchase decision. Insurance may also prove more expensive than for an equivalent saloon car.

29

1.9   Fuel Injection Models

These were pioneered in the early '70s but have only seen widespread introduction since the '80s. Here the carburettor is replaced by a system which relies on an exactly metered amount of fuel being mixed with the correct air volume at the right moment. The benefits include greater fuel efficiency, a cleaner burn (and therefore less harmful exhaust emission), and enhanced reliability and performance.

Fuel-injected models must be maintained properly, and if you are thinking of buying one secondhand, check for a thorough service history; regular servicing with oil and fuel filter changes are important. When driving, be careful not to let the fuel tank drop to zero – dirt and dust sucked into the system can upset its efficiency.

The fuel injection components (which comprise many non-serviceable parts) can be expensive to replace. A point to watch on older secondhand models – those having done say 60,000 to 70,000 miles – is that the fuel pumps and sensors linked to the central control unit can be the first to fail and when this happens the system may go out-of-phase leading to excessive fuel consumption. Generally with fuel injection models the picture is fairly black and white; they work either very well or hardly at all.

1.10 Turbo-charged Models

Turbocharger units are apparatus fitted mainly to top of the range models, in order to improve performance. The unit is fitted to the exhaust system and works by directing air under pressure to the carburettor or fuel-injection unit and, by mixing with more fuel, helps to increase power output. Such engines usually have more robust components especially the pistons, piston rings and exhaust valves to withstand the greater pressures and heating inherent in the system.

When buying a 'turbo' model, check the frequency of the service intervals to date – they should be regular. With serious neglect a turbo unit can disintegrate causing untold damage to the engine. Replacement units can cost around £500 plus labour. Regular engine oil and oil filter changes are critical as is the use of a top quality motor oil, due to the high temperature of a turbo.

TABLE 1: DEFECTS AND FAULTS COMMONLY FOUND IN A CROSS-SECTION OF USED CARS.		FREQ
USED CAR OVER 3 YEARS OLD	USED CAR 6 TO 8 YEARS	(No of Cars)
	EXHAUST OR PART EXHAUST	1 in 2
	PROBLEMS WITH BRAKES — RUST AT PAINT - DAMAGED POINTS	1 in 3
	"INSIDE-OUT" RUSTING; STEERING AND SUSPENSION	1 in 4
EXHAUST OR PART EXHAUST	RUSTING AT SEAMS	1 in 5
BODYWORK SQUEAK	ENGINE MISFIRE OR LEAK BATTERY CLUTCH PAINT SHINE LOSS E EXIDE $^{\circ}P$	1 in 6
RUST AT PAINT - DAMAGED POINTS		1 in 7
E ENGINE PINKING		1 in 8
DOOR LOCKS/HANDLES E ENGINE MISFIRE OR LEAK UNEVEN TYRE WEAR		1 in 9
MS^{-2} ACCELERATION FLAT SPOTS WET RAINWATER SEEPAGE		1 in 10
GEARBOX (ENGAGEMENT) ICE COLD STARTING		1 in 11

1.11   Colour

Colour choice is obviously a personal matter but it is worth noting that bright, light and glossy ones are safer than colours such as black, dark blue, dark grey etc – which tend not to stand out quite so clearly against misty and overcast backgrounds.

> **When considering the eventual re-sale of a car, remember that it is the smaller, mass produced, brightly coloured ones which appear to retain most value.**

You might find the car of your choice but not like the colour. A respray is an option but a quality respray is expensive – a poor finish will severely reduce the car's value, and there is the likelihood of the paintwork cracking, splitting and peeling within perhaps a matter of only a few months. In any case, will the new colour match the interior trim, will you respray in the boot and under the bonnet (extra cost), and will future potential purchasers think the car has been resprayed after an accident or, worse still, stolen?

1.12   Model Upgrades

Car manufacturers frequently upgrade the specification of each model in their ranges, so check to see if the model you are interested in was the last of its range - you may be able to buy a much improved model for only a little extra money.

1.13   Type Of Fuel

Diesel or petrol? In recent years diesel has become a more acceptable fuel for private cars with the advantage that it can give up to 25% more efficiency (it releases its energy more quickly than petrol and also gives a cleaner burn). It is cheaper to refine than petrol and retails for a correspondingly lower price, contains no lead additive and is considered to be more 'friendly' to the environment. Since diesel cars are still a minority you rarely have to queue for long at filling stations. And diesel models are not dependent on the weather for their ability to start. Diesel engines have fewer moving parts and a much longer life expectancy. The disadvantages are that secondhand diesel cars are more costly (due to their more complex engines), are noisier than their petrol-burning counterparts, suffer a loss in performance and the fuel is considered to be somewhat messier to handle than petrol. This has limited their appeal to only a small part of the market. However, diesels are much more popular in Europe which may be an indication of future trends.

1.14   Leaded Or Unleaded?

More and more new cars recently have been manufactured to run on unleaded petrol and, since 1989 all have. Some older cars (as old as fourteen years in fact) are able to run on it either exclusively or mixed with 4-star, e.g. three fills with unleaded and the fourth with leaded; some can be converted to use unleaded with little or no cost, while some cannot be at all, which can make choosing a particular secondhand model that you would prefer to run on unleaded petrol rather complicated. However, let us look briefly at the two types of petrol, and what determines whether or not your potential secondhand choice can be converted to run on unleaded.

Lead is an *additive* which is given to petrol to enhance its performance and to protect engine valves from excessive wear, but which for a long time has been known to cause considerable harm, particularly to children. In 1985 the lead content in petrol was actually reduced without significant loss of performance and in 1986 unleaded petrol, at somewhere between 3 and 4-star rating, gained limited introduction throughout the country. However, while a tremendous breakthrough, unleaded petrol is still perhaps not as environmentally 'friendly' as many of us are conditioned to believe. True, if lead is not actually added to petrol then clearly the air we breathe will be cleaner; but this should really only be considered the first step in reducing widespread exhaust pollution since there are also deadly carcinogens (cancer producing agents) present in petrol, the hydrocarbon benzene for example.

A second step involves the recent introduction of the catalytic converter which, by utilising a ceramic filter in the exhaust system, is able to change the nature of toxic to less harmful (and even safe) emissions. Note that if you buy a car with a catalytic converter you *must* use unleaded petrol to avoid damaging the filter.

It is possible to convert most cars from leaded to unleaded petrol. The main change involves an alteration to the ignition timing but on others the cylinder head may need attention too (because of the amount of lubrication needed) so that for some cars the huge expense involved in making a replacement would make this neither a cheap nor viable option.

Before buying a particluar secondhand model, make a point of asking at an appropriate main dealer garage if conversion will be cheap and straight forward, or even if they will do it free of charge for you. You will need to quote year (age) of the car, engine size and whether it is a fuel-injected model. You will also be told if you need to use a mixture of unleaded and leaded afterwards.

A selling point of unleaded petrol is that it is cheaper than conventional 4-star, but you have to check that the car using unleaded petrol has a similar mpg figure to the car running on 4-star and is not actually using more fuel.

Chapter 2

GENERAL ON USED CARS

Introduction

Before we begin a full structural and mechanical survey on a prospective car, we might learn from what the statistics tell us about the general condition of used cars. In doing so we should uncover the reasons for differences in repair costs for both 'recent' and 'older' models, understand the importance of determining a car's history and former uses and learn how to read a good price guide to maximum effect.

Reliability Report On Used Cars: Common Faults

Included in a very popular consumer magazine published in 1988 (*Which?* magazine) was an article which highlighted the main defects and faults you could expect to find in a range of new and used makes of car. Problems with brand new cars need not concern us here; however, the used cars were those models over three years old and those over six, with models over eight years not considered in the survey. Table 1 represents a summary of that reliability report and identifies the more common components that would need either part or total replacement or that would require some attention, if only cosmetic.

"Recent" Used Cars

With possibly a few exceptions, the methods used to assess the condition of a used car do not depend much on its age, since both young cars (under 5 years) and older ones (over 10 years) operate on much the same structural and mechanical principles.

What you should be building into your spending limit, though, is not only a good idea of the newer car's likely running costs, but also an idea of what it could cost to repair if and when it malfunctions. For older cars (pre-1983, say) many secondhand and reconditioned parts may not be overly expensive and their fitting may quite often be accomplished by the owner. In cars manufactured since around 1985, however, there have been considerable technological advances including the development and widespread introduction of electronic ignition, fuel injection, electronic warning lights, electric mirrors, windows and sunroof, air conditioning, heated front seats and trip computers. While these are great achievements they are by no means essential to comfortable driving, and can make repair not only awkward but very costly – many of the repairs may only be carried out by a main dealer who can afford the necessary specialist equipment. In addition, use of many of these extras contributes to your fuel bill, adding mileage-robbing weight.

As an illustration of the difficulty in replacing even a regular component in a newer car, consider a fan heater arrangement: in some older cars this might be a half hour job due to the accessibility of the part, which is likely to cost in the region of £45-70. In more modern cars the same replacement can cost you up to 12 hours labour, whether it is done by a main dealer or smaller outfit, because the dashboard may have to be completely removed in order to do so. If you consider even the conservative figure of £25 per hour labour, then you can expect this type of job to set you back some

£300-£450. This is not to suggest that repair bills on younger secondhand cars are always going to be astronomical or that they will be dirt cheap on older cars, only that you would do well to examine realistically the possibilities, your requirements and your budget beforehand.

2.1 *What You Are Buying In A Used Car*

You can never be 100% certain that the used car you will buy is going to be great value and even with the benefit of a thorough vehicle inspection you will only be *reducing* the risks, however significantly. After all, it has been known for even brand new cars to have some pretty serious inherent imperfections.

The commodity you are actually buying is the economical life left in the car by the previous owner(s). You could define the "economical life" of a car in terms of the use you can take from it without having to make expensive replacements or repairs outside of normal, regular servicing and maintenance.

When inspecting a car's overall condition and in assessing anything that might need replacing you must bear in mind that the older it is, and the more use that it has had, the more attention it will likely need. However, just because an older car is going to need two new tyres and a replacement gearbox does not necessarily make it a bad buy. As a general rule of thumb, you should expect to spend an amount in putting things right that corresponds to the price you paid for it in the first place. For example, with a car priced at £500-£1,000* (probably a 1976 to 1980 model) you might expect to pay around £500 in repairs that could be of a structural, mechanical or electrical nature. A newer car (1981 to 1986) priced between £1,000 and £4,000* might need an additional 20-30% of this initial outlay to make it serviceable. Repairs on the most recent secondhand cars, built between 1986 and 1989, for which you might have paid in the region of £4,000 to £7,000,* might account for some 10% of this figure. The moral of this is that although the 10% figure quoted for the most recent secondhand cars might be the same as the 50% or more figure in the older ones, the reason you're paying it is because of the longer total life you expect to get out of the latter. And you should make

---

* These figures refer to approximate secondhand price ranges that you might expect for a cross-section of models.

allowance for these kind of figures in your budget.

It is most important to decide in your own mind what it is you are prepared to accept in a used car *before* you buy it, since people's expectations differ enormously. One person may find minor problems a serious let down (one door doesn't shut nicely or the driver's seat is becoming worn); another may perceive this same car to be a perfectly satisfactory aquisition.

Depreciation

One school of thought, quite justifiable in its own way, suggests that you never really get true value for money with a used car when you compare what you take from it with what you have to put back in terms of running costs and repairs. Depreciation is more or less inevitable. Certainly, estimates for the rates of depreciation do vary widely and, while there are rough guidelines as to how much a particular car within a particular class is likely to be worth after a certain amount of use, there are two main reasons why you should not pay too much attention to this. First you are choosing a secondhand car now which you have decided will suit your present and foreseeable future needs and is the best you can afford. Second, it is unlikely that you could begin to predict accurately a resale value any number of years from now, and when the time does come for you to sell your car, you can be sure that the final price will not be fixed and it will be up to the private buyer who, if he wants the car enough, will pay your asking price.

2.2 Determining A Vehicle's History: Former Keepers And Uses

Let us assume that you have spotted a car you like, perhaps on a dealers' forecourt. What should you do first? Well, before going much further with a structural or mechanical survey (covered in a later chapter), and certainly before you think of test driving, you should proceed by asking the dealer/private seller some pointed questions in order to determine the car's history and likely former uses.

Preliminary Checks

Preferably you will address the owner, but a dealer – unless he just bought from an auction – will have some idea of a car's history from the person who traded it in to him. It is in his interest to do so.

> **Ask to see the vehicle registration document and glance at the number of previous owners it has had. If there have been two or three in as many months* then forget the car since for some, probably very expensive, reason each one could not wait to get rid of it quickly enough.**

If the number is acceptable, then make a (mental) note of the last recorded owner's or company's address (you can get their phone number from directory enquiries and call them later if need be). That person should have handed over all the relevant records that he had, including M.O.T. certificates, repair bills and service receipts. If it is not a company car and it is not immediately obvious what it has been used for, then

---

* The vehicle registration document will not directly tell you the recency of all the owner changes, however, this is something that can be found out.

ask. For example, a pool car for the use of everybody in the division of a company – even if registered in one man's name – may have been subject to some pretty flagrant abuse. Likewise if an old lady has used it for her twice-weekly shopping trips two miles down the road, you can expect a multitude of problems to be brewing; including frequent cold starts rapidly wearing away the cylinder bores, high carbon build-up and quickly rotting exhaust. In either of these cases you are likely to land yourself a bad buy but you will have saved yourself any further disappointment by asking the right questions.

Company Cars

Around 13% of all cars presently on the road have been company owned and in 1989 as many as 51% were fleet cars.*

If the car was company owned, then find out how many drivers it had, if more than one. If only one, then try to determine this person's age. A young, aggressive rep. may have given fairly hard treatment to his car. On the other hand a middle-aged driver, especially if he

---

* D.O.T. figure, 1990.

drove something a bit more upmarket, is likely to have treated the car with more respect – something that necessarily would have come from a good few years of driving experience. This is, however, only a generalisation.

Some company cars can be good buys, especially the younger three or four year olds. Regular, long-distance motorway journeys made by a solitary driver means that the car will have been operating at optimal working temperatures thus minimising mechanical wear and tear. Servicing would most certainly have been up to the mark, and any malfunctions would have been spotted and rectified as they occurred. Remember that young company cars have to be that much more dependable than the average private car, for obvious reasons. In the case of a rep.'s car check the interior – the upholstery fabric, carpets, interior trim etc. Do you notice an overall cleanliness or even newness about it? What about the state of the pedals (how worn?), floor pan (is the floor the same colour as the carpet or has it been repainted?); and how about the back seat – has it even been used? Was the boot used much either, and is it clean now? Next the doors; they should hang properly and shut with a characteristic 'clunk'. Check them all.

Check for signs that the car has been used as a taxi or mini-cab: look for evidence of very high mileage, grubby interior, radio or phone attachment points, very worn pedal rubbers and drivers seat, and even a taxi-for-hire sign attachment point. Contact the previous owner(s).

For some companies it may be policy to sell when the car is three years old since they may not want the complications of spending on any parts that might have failed the car its first or subsequent M.O.T.(s). These cars can prove the best buy, since a car of three years old should fly through its M.O.T. Other firms hang onto a car for longer, say seven or eight years from new, until they feel they have got the full 'working' life out of the car and then relinquish it the day that it does give problems.

Do beware of company cars of this age group since, if heavily depreciated, it will be you that picks up the full tab for any of the necessary repairs and replacement parts.

2.3   Mileage

Take a look at the recorded mileage and do not be immediately put off if it seems high since, as we have seen, regular, consistent motorway journeys may have left the car in excellent working condition (along with regular maintenance and good driving habits of course).

"Clocked" Cars

Next you will need to determine whether the mileage on the clock is true. When the mileage display on the milometer is wound back to a lower value, the car is said to be "clocked" and is done to fool you into thinking that the car has travelled several thousand miles fewer than it really has. Clocking takes two forms. Most commonly, the milometer is wound back a few thousand miles, as suggested above, or it is returned to zero mileage. Look very carefully at the figures and study the vehicle registration document. You will see if the mileage tallies roughly with the age of the car and number of owners, or that it at least looks reasonable. For example, a one-owner-from-new car is three years old and has covered 82,000 miles. This is very high mileage (about 27,000 per year – more than double the national average). You would be relieved to find out that this is a company car belonging to one rep. only who was constantly on the road, and in this case the mileage is probably very accurate. Remember that the average annual national mileage is of the order of 12,000. Now suppose you are looking at a ten year old car with three owners and a mileage of 55,000; you would have every reason to be a little more suspicious but don't be hasty in your conclusions – there could be a good reason for it. Incidentally, individuals who clock their own cars will not be breaking the law *as long as this is declared when they sell or trade it in; however, clocking by dealers not only becomes illegal, but also a criminal offence.* (see Chapter 6: Guarantees, Warranties And Your Basic Legal Rights). **A staggering 25% of all used cars are estimated to be clocked.** Check that the row of figures is properly aligned since once a car has been clocked, it is extremely difficult to get all the numbers to reappear in step. For example, consider a car whose milometer reads 68,510 miles:

Fig.1. Milometer (Odometer) readings: Checking for "clocked" mileage.

a)

b)

c)

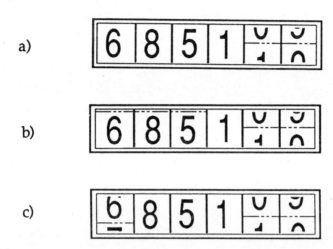

It is only the thousands and tens of thousands mileage columns that you will need to worry about since altering less than 1,000 miles is not going to 'save' very much from the clocker's point of view.

Both a) and b) in Fig.1 look reasonable enough, even without perfect alignment, but in c) the figure '6' especially looks to be quite out of step with the other figures. If this car has been clocked you will not really be sure if it has done 78,000 or even 88,000 miles and you could be gambling on being cheated out of some 20,000+ miles. My advice would be to walk away from a car like this especially if you discover other signs of deceit.

Another clocking ploy is to paint over part of a figure to make it look like a lower number, for example, to make an '8' look like a '3'. You will not necessarily notice this on casual inspection, but imagine your anger when in the case of a milometer recording 63,500 another 500 miles increases the mileage to 69,000!

If in any doubt, telephone the previous owner who will probably talk very freely especially if there is no comeback on it for him. He should at least be able to recall the car's approximate mileage when he finished with it, but if he is cagey you might wonder whether he clocked it himself.

Sometimes a milometer looks as though it has probably been 'zeroed' e.g. a car of three or four years which displays only 3,500 miles. Firstly, look for evidence of tampering with the unit's housing – it would have had to be removed to get to the clock part – and for any scratched or damaged screwheads that might betray a recently removed instrument from the dashboard. However, if changing the milometer has been done for good reason there should be a legitimate receipt to back up anything the seller tells you.

2.4   Documentation

Examine the M.O.T. certificates. The more complete the vehicle's history the better recourse you will have to its true mileage. A five-year-old car will have two M.O.T. certificates and at each one the then-mileage will have been recorded; so check on each one that the interim mileages look feasible for the kind of driving the car will have done. Check the obvious, too, that the present recorded mileage is actually the same or greater than that noted on the latest M.O.T. paper. And definitely forget a car whose log book "cannot be found just now".

Service Records

Service records are another means by which you can determine faithful mileage. In younger cars the service record can take the form of a book which is stamped when the car is serviced at regular intervals, e.g. every 6 months or 6,000 miles is most common. Even when the car is older, some owners keep a dated receipt issued with the service on which the mileage has been recorded (especially in the case of a company who will have spent possibly a lot of time and money on a rep.'s or manager's car). You should always ask to see any records that you think are relevant.

Back to the interior for a moment; you could take a look at the steering wheel pattern which should have worn at a rate commensurate with the mileage. If the steering wheel pattern was of deliberately rough texture at manufacture, is it now 'smoothing' in accordance with 48,000 or 88,000 miles? If it is a popular car then you probably know someone locally who will let you compare it with their own car. Likewise, with pedal rubbers; do they look old and tattered? If these look newish, have the old ones been replaced in order to convey a false impression of the mileage the car has actually covered?

There is a school of thought that questions whether you need be concerned at all about clocking in the case of a ten-year-old car since in nearly all cases the mileage, substantial anyway, is not going to be overly affected by clocking of around 10,000 miles. Even for a car two years old – how much will an extra 10,000 miles affect its future mileage? It is the ones in between that seem to matter the most. However, there is good news for buyers of secondhand vehicles as far as clocked cars go, in that The Motor Trade Consumer Protection Bill (if it goes through Parliament) will aim to give Trading Standards officers increased powers to check for evidence of clocked cars while still on dealers' forecourts. The Bill should come into operation by the early 1990s.

Important Vehicle ID (Identification) Numbers: Stolen Cars

A very quick check you must make while you have the vehicle registration document in your hand is to be satisfied that the registration plates tally and also that the engine and chassis numbers tie up. The first couple of pages in your manual will tell you where to locate these numbers on the car. At the same time check the other details on the form such as colour of body work, engine capacity, trim level of model and transmission type. Any discrepancies could indicate a stolen car or simply that someone has failed to report any vehicle particular changes to the DVLC. Point this out and get the seller to notify the DVLC *before* you buy. This will ensure that you are buying a 'clean' vehicle.

If you are unfortunate enough to have bought a 'hot' (i.e stolen) car, remember that there is very limited recourse even in innocence. The police, when they trace it, will impound the car and you risk losing all your money unless you sue the person who sold it to you – if you can find him. The only real safeguards are to check engine and chassis numbers, and the name on the registration document. Ask to see the original bill of sale or other ID if necessary.

Vehicle Registration

When checking the number plate details and that the single letter suffix or prefix does correspond with the age of the car (a list of registration suffix and prefix letters for 1963-1993 is given in Fig.2), look at the other three-letter sequence in the registration number. It will tell you where the vehicle was first registered; the second two letters (the first is a serial letter) will indicate the town, city or district of registration of the car. Occasionally you can tell a little of the car's history from this; if you buy a car with a three-letter registration series 'PYY', for instance, the 'YY' indicates registration in Central London. If the log book records the addresses of the one, two or three previous owners as being in Central London also, then you might assume that the car has been used there for the major part of its life. Such a car would have been driven in mainly stop/start traffic and you could fairly reason that a car driven in a more open, rural area is going to be much more healthy. A minor point, however, this is all part of the procedure of thoroughly investigating a vehicle's former uses and history which, you must now begin to appreciate, will require a little bit of organised effort on your part if you are to minimise your risk of buying anything that is less than good value for money. A list of two-letter London registration codes is reproduced in Fig.3.

Registration Number Plates

Since 1963 a five to seven digit sequence has been used on car registration plates. Cars registered between 1st January and 31st December would have carried a suffix letter 'A', e.g. TGF 609A and for cars in 1964 the suffix letter in newly registered vehicles would have been 'B', e.g. UBB 218B. In 1967 the new registration date was changed to 1st August, such that an 'F' registered car would have been so between 1.8.67 and 31.7.68. Excluding the letters I*, O, Q*, U and Z*, letters were used progressively through the alphabet until 'Y' and then the age of a car would be denoted by a prefix letter starting with 'A' on 1.8.83, e.g. A418 TUW.

Fig.2. Registration suffix and prefix letters for cars 1963-1993

(Suffixes)

A	1.1.63 to 31.12.63	B	1.1.64 to 31.12.64
C	1.1.65 to 31.12.65	D	1.1.66 to 31.12.66
E	1.1.67 to 31.7.67	F	1.8.67 to 31.7.68
G	1.8.68 to 31.7.69	H	1.8.69 to 31.7.70
J	1.8.70 to 31.7.71	K	1.8.71 to 31.7.72
L	1.8.72 to 31.7.73	M	1.8.73 to 31.7.74
N	1.8.74 to 31.7.75	P	1.8.75 to 31.7.76

* Letters I and Z are used for registering cars in both Northern Ireland and The Republic of Ireland, e.g. 'RZB' would indicate a registration in Cork and 'RIP' would show a car registered in Kilkenny. The letter Q implies a 'kit' car or one whose original registration details are missing, or unconventional.

R	1.8.76 to 31.7.77	S	1.8.77 to 31.7.78
T	1.8.78 to 31.7.79	V	1.8.79 to 31.7.80
W	1.8.80 to 31.7.81	X	1.8.81 to 31.7.82
Y	1.8.82 to 31.7.83		

(Prefixes)

A	1.8.83 to 31.7.84	B	1.8.84 to 31.7.85
C	1.8.85 to 31.7.86	D	1.8.86 to 31.7.87
E	1.8.87 to 31.7.88	F	1.8.88 to 31.7.89
G	1.8.89 to 31.7.90	H	1.8.90 to 31.7.91
J	1.8.91 to 31.7.92	K	1.8.92 to 31.7.93

Fig.3. A list of two-letter registration sequences for London-registered cars.

CENTRAL LONDON
HM (e.g.CHM 311T), HV, HX, JD, UC, UL, UU, UV, UW, YE, YF, YH, YK, YL, YM, YN, YO, YP, YR, YT, YU, YV, YW, YX, YY

SOUTH LONDON

GC (e.g. AGC 987W), GF, GH, GJ, GK, GN, GO, GP, GT, GU, GW, GX, GY, MV, MX, MY

NORTH LONDON

BY (e.g. D48 SBY), LA, LB, LC, LD, LE, LF, LH, LK, LL, LM, LN, LO, LP, LR, LT, LU, LW, LX, LY, RK, OY, MC, MD, ME, MF, MG, MH, MK, ML, MM, MP, MT, MU

2.5 Summary

Determining a car's history is quite a tricky task. The signs are there but if you are to learn anything of value you must remember to use every available piece of information before concluding anything. **Never conclude anything about a used car from isolated observations.**

In general, when considering a car's history, you should do the following:

- Ask to see both the vehicle registration and M.O.T. certificates and check the frequency and recency of its owners; make a note of the last owner's name and address.

- Ask to see any service and repair or maintenance bills – they can help confirm the true mileage.

- Ask about the car's previous uses if not already obvious.

- Approximately 10-13% of cars are or have been company-owned. When considering one of these, try to determine the number and ages of the drivers *and* the type of firm that owned it and why they are selling it *now*.

- Do not be put off by a high mileage car – provided regular service, maintenance and repair history is in order you could get a good buy – as you will pay less than you would for a car with average mileage.

- Check the interior for signs of wear commensurate with mileage, including pedal rubbers, steering wheel pattern, gear stick handle upholstery, interior velour and trim, back seats, boot area and doors.

- Check if the car is "clocked" by noting obvious misalignment of mileage gauge figures (Fig.1); extremely low mileages (zero-ing); painted-over numbers; tampered-with speedometer unit.

- Check current mileage against previous M.O.T. certificates and refuse a car whose registration and M.O.T. details "cannot be found".

- Check that the engine and chassis numbers tally with what is recorded on the registration document and also other details including bodywork colour, engine capacity, number plates and date of registration.

- Investigate the district, town or city of registration and address(es) of the previous owners – find out what you can about the car's life to date.

- Try to find out if the car has been 'garaged' at the end of each day's driving – this would have left it in much better condition with minimal corrosion.

2.6   What A Used Car Price Guide Will Tell You

Used car price guides can be a very useful starting point when investigating the "going" price of a secondhand car, whether you are buying privately, from a dealer or from auction. They are also the best place to start when you are thinking of selling your own car and are in any case far more reliable than most colleagues' ill-informed guesswork.

In addition to the used car price sections found in some motoring magazines, there are two main guides to choose from: *Parker's Car Price Guide* and *The Motorists Guide*, both retailing for around £1.50 and available monthly. While both claim to be Britain's No. 1 guide, *Parker's* does list in excess of 82,500 prices and also a comprehensive list of auction sites which includes their telephone numbers and auction starting times, with even a 'tip' section on how to bid. Both guides also list prices of brand new cars.

Categorisation

Both guides list cars according to make and at the beginning of each model is a brief history that details the months and years of significant improvement to the model (see Fig.4).

The oldest registrations covered by either guide – depending on type of car of course – are mainly 'W' and

'X' (1981) and when listing prices for current used models both rate according to: new, A1 or first class, good, fair or average, and trade prices; and there is a good description of how you should use these definitions to assess a car's condition. Of the two, possibly *Parker's* bolder columns make identifying the necessary figures that much easier, yet *The Motorists Guide* provides more accessible length and width dimensions of the car with mileages based on differing yearly averages (see Fig.4). Both indicate a car's insurance group rating – very helpful when thinking of switching to a different make or model.

On the whole, both are compact mines of useful information and are a must for any secondhand buyer wanting the very best deal.

Fig.4. (Overleaf) Is a comparison of the information obtainable from two of the major price guides: The Renault 14.

Fig.4. A comparison of the information obtainable from two of the major price guides: The Renault 14

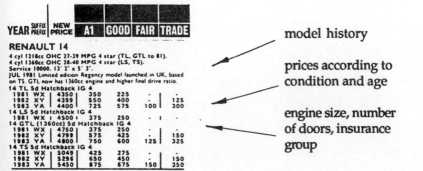

MOTORISTS GUIDE

Year Regd	New Price	Reg Lets.	Mlge 000s	1st Class	Good Cond	Mlge 000s	Avge Cond	Trade Avge

RENAULT

continued

14
4 cyl 75 x 69 mm 1218 cc OHC, GTL (1977/81) and TL
4 cyl 75 x 77 mm 1360 cc OHC-TS, LS and GTL (Sep 81 on)
Oct 80. GTL/TS models continued addn warning lights low fuel, etc, and new illuminated switches on 14 TS console
July 81. Limited edition 'Regency' available, based on TS using same 1360 cc power unit. Total cost new £5135
Sep 81. GTL Saloon fitted with 1360 cc engine, replacing 1218 cc unit.
Optional extras: (1983) Sunroof (GTL/TS) £206, Metallic Paint £52

GTL HATCHBACK (1218 cc) 5dr O/L 13' 2" W 5' 4" Ins Gp 4 (all)

Year	New Price	Reg Lets	Mlge	1st Class	Good Cond	Mlge	Avge Cond	Trade
1981	4492	W&X 78		700	450	93	325	175
(1360 cc)								
1982	4799	X&Y 71		950	825	86	475	300
1983	4800	Y&A 66		1150	825	79	675	500

TS HATCHBACK (1360 cc) 5dr O/L 13' 2" W 5' 4" Ins Gp 4

1981	5049	W&X 78		775	475	93	325	175
1982	5298	X&Y 71		1050	700	86	525	325
1983	5450	Y&A 66		1325	950	79	750	550

model history

prices according to condition, mileage and age

engine size, number of doors, → dimensions, insurance group

PARKER'S GUIDE

YEAR SUFFIX PREFIX	NEW PRICE	A1	GOOD	FAIR	TRADE

RENAULT 14
4 cyl 1218cc OHC 27-39 MPG 4 star (TL, GTL to 81).
4 cyl 1360cc OHC 28-40 MPG 4 star (LS, TS).
Service 10000. 13' 2" x 5' 3".
JUL 1981 Limited edition Regency model launched in UK, based on TS. GTL now has 1360cc engine and higher final drive ratio.

14 TL 5d Hatchback IG 4

Year	Price	A1	Good	Fair	Trade
1981 WX	4350	350	225	.	125
1982 XY	4399	550	400	100	300
1983 YA	4400	725	575	100	300

14 LS 5d Hatchback IG 4

| 1981 WX | 4500 | 375 | 250 | . | . |

14 GTL (1360cc) 5d Hatchback IG 4

1981 WX	4750	375	250	.	
1982 XY	4799	575	425	.	150
1983 YA	4800	750	600	125	325

14 TS 5d Hatchback IG 4

1981 WX	5049	425	275	.	
1982 XY	5296	650	450	.	150
1983 YA	5450	875	675	150	350

model history

prices according to condition and age

engine size, number of doors, insurance group

Chapter 3

WHAT TO LOOK FOR – STRUCTURALLY AND MECHANICALLY

Introduction

It is not possible to examine every single working (or non-working) part of a car – there are too many of them and there is never enough time. Often it is the case that your anticipated driving life with the car makes a little surface rust, accident damage, or some worn elements of the engine insignificant in relation to the price you will be paying.

As a rule you do get what you pay for and although any final decision as to what is or is not acceptable will vary from one individual to the next, with any secondhand car you must expect to pay something towards the replacement of parts. However, you will not want a car that needs too much attention initially, nor one that is going to demand regular bonnet-up treatment, with frequent and high garage repair bills.

The following, while similar to what you might expect to be covered in the course of a vehicle inspection, have been selected as relatively simple tests you can do yourself to make a judgement on a used car.

Note: Certain components vary in both appearance and location in different makes and model of car and so it is advisable to buy or borrow a handbook *specific* to the model you are interested in, in order to make their identification easier when conducting the following tests.

A good guide to get is one of the *Haynes* series which retails for around £8.00 from any good motor factor. Do not rule out, however, the likelihood of picking up the very copy you need from a car boot sale for as little as 35p – I picked up the manual for my present car for only 50p!

3.1   Structural Pointers

General Impression

In trying to decide how a car has been previously treated, you can gather a surprising amount of detail from an inspection of the bodywork alone. You should take a walk around the car observing its overall condition and any obvious dents and rusting. Remember that you are not buying a new car and that it is possible at least one of the panels has been either resprayed, repaired or even replaced. If a good job has been done this matters little, but a bad job not only looks tacky but will lose you money when you come to resell.

Beware of a car that looks too clean and low-priced for its age – it could be hiding serious faults.

Rust

Cars registered and driven exclusively in the North of Britain have a reputation for being somewhat rustier than those in the South due to colder winters and subsequent excesses of salt on the road which assists the corrosion process. Also, certain makes of car have a tendency to rust excessively; purchasing one could be asking for trouble.

Serious rusting at structural points can not only mean an M.O.T. failure but can also make the repair of the car so costly that you may even have to scrap it.

Make sure you examine the following points when checking for rust:

- under front and rear bumpers
- valance area
- door panels and sills
- wheel arches
- front and rear wings
- boot lid/tailgate
- petrol tank
- chassis
- floor pan
- roof
- door seams
- suspension mountings

69

- jack points
- roof and bonnet edges

  and any exposed interface between two welded points. (See Figs.5 and 6)

Filler

There are always signs that filler has been used and you will want to test the extent of it. Tap a part of a panel that you suspect has been filled and if you hear a dull thud rather than a metallic clang you have your answer. A better way is to use a simple magnet which will cling to metal (except aluminium) but not to a filled patch of bodywork. Halfords stock a device known as 'Spotrot' which is basically a magnet with a scale that gives a high reading when held to sound metal, a medium reading near to hidden rust and a low reading where filler is found. The device, which retails for around £7, is able to detect layers of repaint.

The other point to remember about filler work is that bad winters tend to show it up by eating around it and thus leaving the area open to further corrosion.

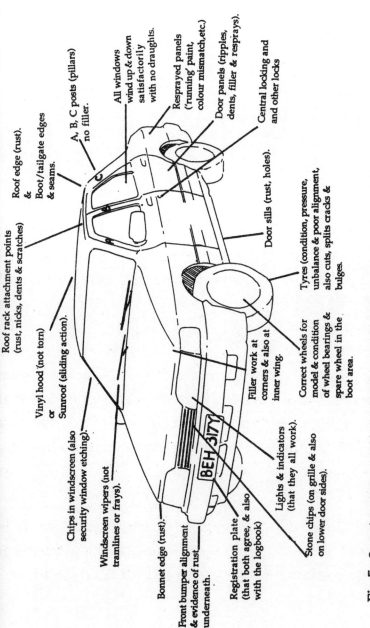

Roof edge (rust).
&
Boot/tailgate edges & seams.

A, B, C posts (pillars)
no filler.

All windows wind up & down satisfactorily with no draughts.

Resprayed panels ('running' paint, colour mismatch, etc.).

Door panels (ripples, dents, filler & resprays).

Central locking and and other locks

Roof rack attachment points (rust, nicks, dents & scratches)

Vinyl hood (not torn)
or
Sunroof (sliding action).

Door sills (rust, holes).

Tyres (condition, pressure, unbalance & poor alignment, also cuts, splits cracks & bulges.

Chips in windscreen (also security window etching).

Windscreen wipers (not tramlines or frays).

Filler work at corners & also at inner wing.

Correct wheels for model & condition of wheel bearings & spare wheel in the boot area.

Bonnet edge (rust).

Front bumper alignment & evidence of rust underneath.

Registration plate (that both agree, & also with the logbook)

Lights & indicators (that they all work).

Stone chips (on grille & also on lower door sides).

BEH 317V

Fig.5. Some important considerations when determining a car's overall condition

Fig.6. Important points to examine with the vehicle on a hoist.

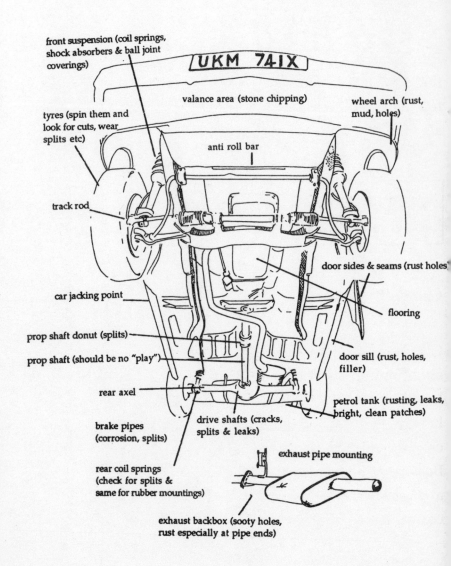

front suspension (coil springs, shock absorbers & ball joint coverings)

UKM 741X

valance area (stone chipping)

wheel arch (rust, mud, holes)

tyres (spin them and look for cuts, wear splits etc)

anti roll bar

track rod

door sides & seams (rust holes)

car jacking point

flooring

prop shaft donut (splits)

prop shaft (should be no "play")

door sill (rust, holes, filler)

rear axel

petrol tank (rusting, leaks, bright, clean patches)

brake pipes (corrosion, splits)

drive shafts (cracks, splits & leaks)

exhaust pipe mounting

rear coil springs (check for splits & same for rubber mountings)

exhaust backbox (sooty holes, rust especially at pipe ends)

Sills

Run your hands underneath and along the length of the door sills, tapping at close intervals and listening for 'dead sounds' that might betray rust or filler. Feel also for holes caused by rusting at an advanced stage.

> **Check the inner sill; you need to lift up the carpet inside the car by the driver's seat.**

HOT TIP

Chassis

Check for dents and also for any signs that a serious shunt might have reached this far. Chassis rails run the length of the car and must be right and so any damage here will upset the car's balance making it drive off-centre which will be obvious during a test drive. Beware of filler in the visible part. It is possible to have a chassis straightened but you will not want to have to correct this kind of problem before you start.

Floorings

Check underneath the front half of the car for floor corrosion and general damage. Feel for dirt and holes as well and for anything that feels like freshly, or unevenly applied underbody sealant.

Also check the rear half of the floor and the boot floor, in particular for rippling that may have been caused by an accident.

Damp carpets suggest a possible windscreen or sunroof leak.

Wheel   Arches

> Again, feel for holes and rust in every
> crevice, especially at places where mud will
> have lodged (water and salt in it will quickly
> eat away at metal). Gently peel away at any
> loose layers and be reassured if you find
> good metal early on. If layer after layer of
> rust just crumbles away then much of the
> area is rotten and probably beyond repair.

Doors

Look for obvious rusting or filler work that could
indicate crash damage. If not done properly, filled work
shows up as light scratch lines. Look for obvious colour
mismatches between adjacent panels, and also for
patchy respraying or stripes on door panels that do not
line up exactly (Fig.7). Make sure you do this in the
right light – a dealer may try to conceal a mismatched
panel by parking the car in the shade. Doors should
'hang' properly so check the hinges on each door in

turn. Badly closing doors may point to a collision at some time, or may just be a question of needing adjustment. *Study the door panels for signs of paint blistering or bubbling – this is often rust starting from the inside and working its way out. With the doors open, look and feel along the edges and undersides for rust, holes, or any gaps between the inside and outside surfaces of the panel.* Finally, check each of the door locks, and if they are controlled by a central locking mechanism that all doors respond satisfactorily to it.

Fig.7. Important visual checks.

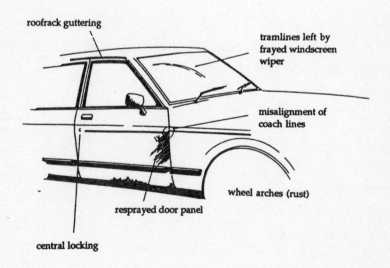

roofrack guttering

tramlines left by frayed windscreen wiper

misalignment of coach lines

wheel arches (rust)

resprayed door panel

central locking

Other Panels

Look for filler and resprayed wing surfaces in particular – the corners of any car are the most vulnerable to damage.

Turn next to the tailgate or boot area and note any colour differences (often a respray implies a replacement panel here). Examine the tailgate and carefully scan for paint that might have run during respray and also for local areas that are either flecked with the 'new' colour or else missed, perhaps betraying the car's original finish. There is always evidence of respraying if you look hard enough. Stand back and check to see if the rear bumper is straight since replacements are not always aligned properly, and just behind the bumper, check for gaps at any seams where spot-welding has been carried out. These will be the first to rust. Lastly, crouch down and look along the length of the car's bodywork for tiny dents in any of the panels (possibly caused by passing traffic or roadside hedges!) which are not so easily noticed when looking at the panel head-on.

Pillars

> Check the windscreen, door and rear pillars (A, B and C posts, respectively – see Fig.5); these do contribute to the integral structure of the bodywork and any filler found here is likely to be quite dangerous since it could cause folding even in a low speed collision. Check at the lower half of the windscreen pillar for peeling lacquer. It could be corrosion, but more seriously might betray the true extent of a hard shunt.

Inner Panels

Open the bonnet and compare the shape and symmetry of the inner wings. Any rust, rippling or filler here must indicate a collision to either the front of the car or its wings (and you ought to take a second look at the visible part of the chassis bars for damage). Also, look at the front bumper alignment, and check whether either of the headlight lenses looks recently renewed.

Finally, look at the front grille, valance area and lower parts of the door panels for stone chip marks. This will tell you if the car has been driven on the motorway a great deal. Bad stone-chipping can leave the metalwork vulnerable to rusting.

Engine Mountings

While the bonnet is open, lean over and take a look down the sides of the engine for the mountings, which look like small rubber doughnuts. They help minimise vibration and should not be cracked or split and ordinarily should last some 12-15 years.

3.2   Mechanical Pointers

Here the picture is less clear cut and your decision to buy is more likely to be swayed by overall condition than by any one single feature of the car in question. For the purpose of this section, mechanical parts are considered to be anything that will wear out and need replacing during the normal course of a car's driving life.

Engine

Get someone else to start the engine for you while you stand at the back with an eye on the exhaust emissions (at the same time, notice how quickly and easily the engine turns over). Blue exhaust points to wear of the piston rings and valve guides. Black clouds mean that either too rich a petrol mixture, or that petrol and oil are being burned. After running the engine for a few minutes, lift up the bonnet and look for oil escaping - in vapour form – from the filler cap region, dipstick or breather valves. A glance at the mileage will tell you if this is an old engine (perhaps 75,000 miles or more) or one that has been prematurely abused.

Replacement Engines

You may decide that it is only the engine which needs replacing. With an older secondhand car it is unlikely you are going to want to pay main dealer prices (£500 £2000) for a reconditioned engine, unless this car is going to mean something to you. There are several other places offering reconditioned engines; however the first thing you should decide is whether or not you are actually getting one that's reconditioned **or** rebuilt. Price is quite a good guide in this and, according to some dealers of reclaimed engines, there can be considerable difference. Generally, a rebuilt engine will not carry a guarantee since it is only the parts that needed it that are actually replaced. In reconditioned engines, however, you can be fairly sure that all parts have been dealt with, including: the crankshaft, connecting rods, gaskets, piston rings, timing belts, valve guides and also the reboring of cylinders and proper machining of any parts that need it. As a result you should get a 12,000 mile or one year guarantee against any major faults. And finally, if you are considering getting a 'new' engine put in, you would be better off using a member of the FER, the Federation of Engine Remanufacturers who have to observe strict standards; their address is given on page 151.

General Running

With the engine on tick-over, listen to its general tone – and of course, the more experience you have had of hearing the difference between good and bad engines the easier it will be. Listen out for too fast a tick-over speed but mainly listen for an even sound with no misfiring. Beware of 'lumpy' sounding engines.

Oil leaks

Engine leaks are usually self-evident, yet finding their source is not always as straightforward since whole areas of the engine can be awash with oils. Leaks will manifest themselves at the weakest points. (For more specific advice see Chapter 9: The Eight Things You Should Do Immediately On Buying a Used Car (If You Want To Save A Lot Of Money)).

Carburettor

If you know that the engine has been professionally tuned recently, you will know that the carburettor has had some attention. Again, with the engine on tick-over, depress the accelerator in a series of short bursts in order to test its response. There should be rapid revs instantly and any delay with the revs will indicate an acceleration 'flat spot'.

Ignition

Examine the high tension (HT or ignition) leads which connect to each spark plug and look for any that are frayed or dirty. Make sure that the spark plugs are not coated in oil, then remove the distributor cap and determine that the 'pick-up' points inside are clean and that the rotor arm arrangement (refer to manual or handbook and see Fig.8) is not badly blackened or burnt out. These items should all be in A1 condition if the car has had a recent service.

Ignition Warning Light

This should come on and go out immediately the engine fires. If it stays on (or comes on later) it can point to: a low battery or alternator or perhaps short circuitry.

Head Gasket

This gasket makes a gas and liquid-tight seal between the engine cylinder head and engine block.

Fig.8. Components of the Ignition System

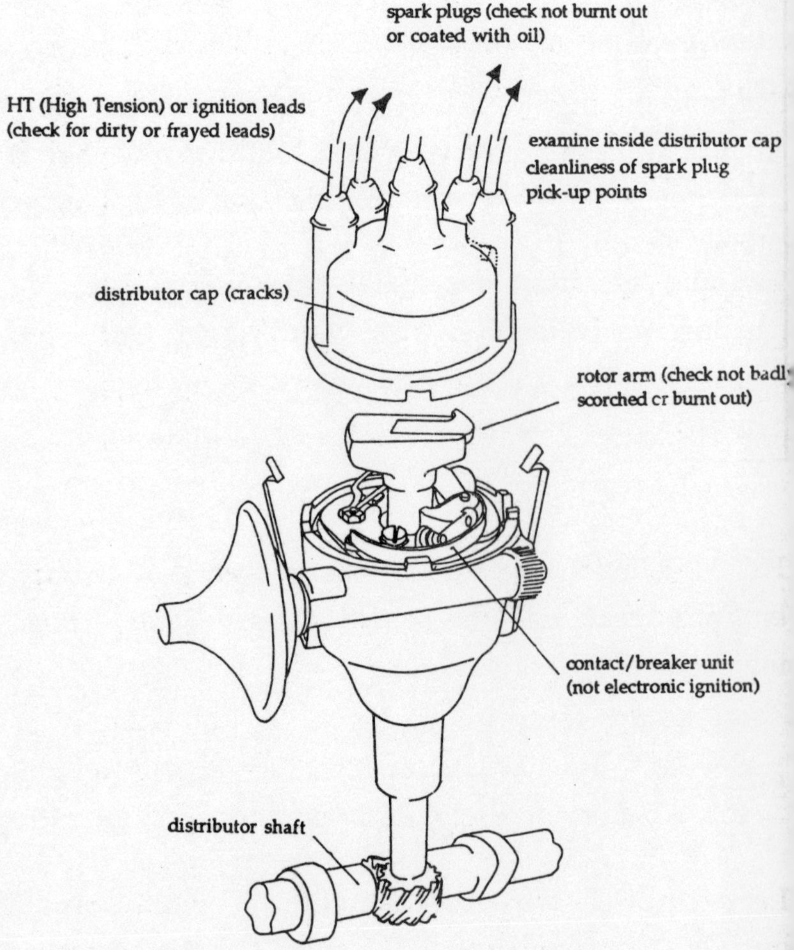

spark plugs (check not burnt out
or coated with oil)

HT (High Tension) or ignition leads
(check for dirty or frayed leads)

examine inside distributor cap
cleanliness of spark plug
pick-up points

distributor cap (cracks)

rotor arm (check not badl
scorched cr burnt out)

contact/breaker unit
(not electronic ignition)

distributor shaft

Overheating can cause it to split and leak, signs of which are a high engine temperature reading (needle approaching the red), continuous thick white exhaust smoke, the presence of white mush under the oil filler cap and on the engine oil dipstick, and/or many bubbles in and around the latter; also radiator water which is low or feels oily. You would have to confirm all of these observations before inferring the problem.

Head gasket replacement on the larger, more complex engines (such as V6's) can be very costly due to inaccessability to that area.

Steering

Lean through the driver's window while standing outside the car and rotate the steering wheel from side to side watching the front offside wheel turning. There should be no visible slack or audible 'clunking' of the steering wheel – you should notice both road and steering wheel move in unison.

Power Steering

A second fan belt will usually tell you that the model is equipped with power steering, and here you are listening for a noisy steering pump which manifests itself as a grumbling sound when the steering wheel is at full lock. This is the kind of sound with which you really need to be familiar; however, when test driving, the main things to notice are whether the steering appears to move in uneven jerks or whether it feels as if you are driving around on flat tyres. Power steering fluid should be red-coloured (not brown) and also up to the mark on its dipstick (a screw cap in the top of the powersteering fluid reservoir). It is also worth mentioning that power steering does have an adverse effect on tyre life.

Clutch

You can do a simple test with the clutch to determine whether or not it is slipping. With the engine running *and handbrake on*, depress the clutch and select third or fourth gear (which will put load on the engine) and, with the revs rising only slightly, raise the clutch as if to pull away: if the engine does not stall immediately, then the clutch is slipping. Repeat this test when the engine is warm. More important for the test drive, satisfy yourself that the clutch engages smoothly as you change gear and, particularly on inclines when changing down, note whether the engine revs rise but without an immediate increase in acceleration. This is tell-tale of a slipping clutch. Also when driving there should be no rattling, clonking, juddering or grinding sounds when engaging the clutch.

Alternator

To check that it is passing on charge to the battery, testing is best done in a darkened area, such as inside a garage. With the engine on tick-over and gearbox in neutral, put the lights on to main beam and increase the engine revs. The headlights should become correspondingly brighter as witnessed by the reflection from the wall. Check too that the alternator fan belt is not slack.

Brakes

If the brakes are servo-assisted (this means that the engine provides help with brake pressure), stand by the open bonnet with the engine running, while somebody operates the brake pedal. As the pedal is released, you should not hear any fizzing, hissing or crackling sounds coming from the master cylinder/servo arrangement (refer to handbook). A test for brake condition is given in Chapter 4.1. The next thing to test is brake effectiveness at both low and high speeds and also during an emergency stop. While on a slope, check the handbrake's holding ability (in an automatic, engage neutral or N when testing the handbrake).Test also the parking brake, P on the automatic gearbox gear shift, and in this case making sure the handbrake is off. Identify and feel the brake pipes underneath the car for corrosion or splits (see Fig.6).

Servo Unit

With the engine and hand brakes off, pump the brake pedal several times and press the pedal to the floor.

Switch the engine on and the brake pedal should dip slightly. This confirms the servo unit is working.

Drive Shafts

Drive shafts transmit the power to the rear wheels on a rear wheeldrive car, to the front wheels on a front wheel drive car, and to all four wheels on a four-wheel drive car, from the differentials/gearbox.

Check to see that there are no cracks or splits or visible grease which would indicate leaking (refer to Fig.9a).

Propeller Shafts

This runs from the gearbox to the back axle on rear wheel drive and four wheel drive cars, transmitting power from the engine. Some cars get through them more quickly than others. Examine the universal joints (or rubber couplings) for splits. With excessive wear, you are likely to experience 'clunking' and eventually intolerable vibrations that may reduce your speed substantially. There should be no play in the shafts at all (see Fig.9b).

Fig.9a. Propeller shaft.

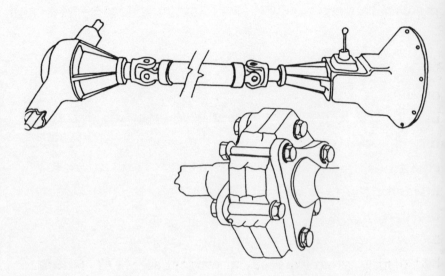

Fig.9b. Drive shaft.

to gearbox
or diff

to wheel

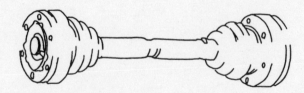

Exhaust

While a stainless steel exhaust may last a fair amount of the car's lifetime, those made of mild steel will usually give you only two or three years service. Every time a car is started from cold, the burning of petrol creates acidic gases, salts and water which eat at the inside of the exhaust material and it is for this reason that frequent, short journeys corrode an exhaust much more quickly than long, uninterrupted ones. Visibly bad rusting on an exhaust can warrant an M.O.T. failure and you will have to make a replacement sooner rather than later. What you will be checking for is that there is at least some life left in it. A blowing exhaust will seriously increase your petrol consumption so to check for leaks, run the engine and cover the exhaust tail pipe with a piece of rolled up rag: if there are no leaks the engine should stall shortly afterwards (exhaust gases will escape anywhere there are holes, which would by now appear sooty). Get the car up on a ramp if possible and when the exhaust is cold, look and feel closely at pipe bends and metal joins (Fig.6). Check the security of exhaust mountings to ensure that the pipe does not rattle or get over-stressed as you are driving, and also that the emissions are reasonably quiet and smooth. Gummy or dry deposits in the tailpipe point to oil burning and fuel system ills, respectively. A final check to carry out: ensure that the boot or tailgate and all windows and vents are shut, and do a sufficiently long test drive to notice whether you can smell or notice any signs of exhaust emission (feeling of drowsiness).

Wheel Bearings

This test is best done with the wheels jacked up, but even if on the road, hold each of the front wheels in turn with both hands and rock them backwards and forwards. If you can move them more than about 1/8" you will probably feel a definite click or vibration which will indicate that the wheel bearings need either adjusting or replacment. During a test drive, you will notice that worn wheel bearings are noisy.

Towbar

Buying a car already equipped with a towbar is not necessarily an indication that the engine has continually pulled heavy loads – but you **must** assume so. Conversely, it may have been factory-fitted yet, to date, unused. Find out from the owner. If you intend to use the car for boating or caravanning, the fitting will save you money.

Suspension

A crude yet reasonable test for the shock absorbers is the well-known 'bounce' test in which, with the car on level ground, you push down quite hard on each wing corner in turn. The wing should then rise, dip slightly, rise again, then come to rest. Continued bouncing will mean that your shock absorbers need replacing. To maintain the car's proper balance, you should get them replaced a pair at a time.

Coil Springs

Again if you can observe the rear springs while standing under a professional hoist, then all the better (Fig.6). If the spring part is actually broken then the car will behave as if there was no spring there at all and, under load, the car will sag making steering and cornering dangerous. This is both an M.O.T. failure and illegal. As with shock absorbers, one broken spring is best replaced by a pair of them in order to maintain the car's proper balance. And while not an M.O.T. failure in itself, you should check that the springs' rubber mountings are not split.

Ball Joint And Ball Joint Coverings

These are vital components of the steering/suspension mechanism which may need renewing if the steering appears sloppy. Even splitting of the rubber coverings would constitue an M.O.T. failure. They are not normally a great expense to replace.

Tyres

Tyres make up such an important part of the car's safety that they deserve some extra attention here. First of all, make sure that the car you are looking at has tyres suitable for it (and preferably all the same brand), since the car's manoeuvering and roadholding characteristics